CW00818900

LAGARTERA
EMBROIDERY

LAGARTERA
EMBROIDERY

and Stitches from Spain

SALLYMILNER
PUBLISHING

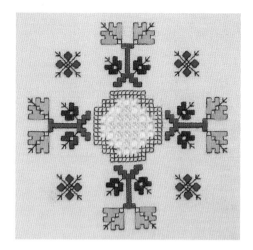

Front cover: detail from an example of Dove's eye filling by Jill Wadsworth

First published in 2003 by
Sally Milner Publishing Pty Ltd
PO Box 2104
Bowral NSW 2576
AUSTRALIA

© The Embroiderers' Guild of South Australia Inc.

Tel: (08) 8234 1104
Fax: (08) 8234 1513
Email: embguild@tne.net.au
Internet: www.embguildsa.org.au

Design by Vivien Valk, 1 bluedog design
Illustrations by Christine Bishop, Lis Steinmetz, Carol Young
Stitch diagrams by Anna Warren, Warren Ventures
Photography by Tim Connolly
Edited by Kathryn Lamberton

Printed in China

National Library of Australia
Cataloguing-in-Publication data:

Lagartera embroidery and stitches from Spain.

Bibliography.
ISBN 1 86351 308 6.

1. Embroidery. I. South Australian Embroiderers' Guild.

746.44

All rights reserved. No part of this publication may be reproduced, stored in
a retrieval system, or transmitted in any form or by any means, electronic,
mechanical, photocopying, recording or otherwise, without prior permission
of the copyright owners and publishers.

10 9 8 7 6 5 4 3 2 1

CONTENTS

FRANCE

SPAIN

● Madrid

• *Toledo*

PORTUGAL

MOROCCO

INTRODUCTION

Embroiderers have been spoiled by the wealth of embroidery literature available to them. On library shelves project-based books and more technical works sit side-by-side with historical studies on this subject. Indeed, there are very few embroidery techniques that have not been studied and re-introduced in either contemporary or traditional form.

This book has grown from a desire of the Publications Committee of The Embroiderers' Guild of South Australia Inc. to reintroduce techniques which have been forgotten in modern publications. One of these comes from the region of Lagartera in Spain.

A Coats publication, Lagartera Embroidery, published in the early 1960's, is one of the few English language references available.

A class in Lagartera embroidery held during The Embroiderers' Guild of South Australia Inc. 1999 National Embroiderers' Conference created unexpected interest and led us to believe that a book on this embroidery would appeal to those keen to learn about this technique. And so our book, Lagartera Embroidery: Stitches from Spain, was born.

A particular feature of Lagartera is that the outlined satin stitch may be accompanied by motifs of drawn thread work, with dove's eye stitch used to create patterns.

The motifs are filled with counted satin stitch, with double running stitch sometimes providing an outline.

Pieces made entirely of drawn thread work can also be found; however, complex work like this has not been included in this publication. The focus of this book is traditional designs and contemporary developments of these designs based on counted satin and double running stitch.

The Historical embroideries featured at the back of the book demonstrate the Lagartera technique, while the piece from Romania in which the similarities to Lagartera are apparent has been included for interest.

Mulberry Mat by Gay Sanderson adapted from a historic Roumanian mat

HISTORICAL NOTES

Lagartera (pronounced La ghar te rah), a colourful peasant embroidery traditionally worked on hand-woven linen, originated in a Spanish village of the same name.

Historic documents indicate that La Villa de Lagartera was founded and settled as early as the twelve hundreds. Similar documents establish that the traditions which led to the Lagartera-style of fine embroidered goods dates from the sixteenth century when excellent embroiderers from Lagartera went to the nearby village of Oropesa 'to sew exquisitely embroidered patterns on clothing and linens' for the Dona Juana, Countess of Toledo …

> Women from Lagartera, undoubtedly influenced by the Arabic designs and arabesque patterns adopted during centuries of Islamic occupation, wove their patterns into clothes, … sheets and pillowcases, bedspreads … and wall hangings …*
>
> A young woman's dowry would contain many pieces of this embroidery, which was characterised by lively colours and geometric motifs suggestive of Moorish influence, so that animal motifs are rarely seen.

Lagartera is worked on an even-weave linen using satin stitch, which is often outlined in Spanish stitch (now known as double running stitch, or Holbein stitch). Traditionally, black or brown thread was used to give a strong outline.

* *Direccion General de Turismo, Comercio y Artesania. Asociacion Profesional de Artesanos de las Labores de Lagartera.*

Historic Roumanian Mat

The earliest known examples of double running stitch are to be found on linen fragments uncovered during archaeological excavations in Egypt and believed to have been worked at some time between the thirteenth and fifteenth centuries. It is known that this stitch was used in many Islamic countries and other areas of the Mediterranean.

The appearance of double running stitch in Spain is thought to have been the result of trade between the Moors and the Egyptians and the Muslim settlements in Spain. In an early sixteenth-century publication in Germany, Arabic double running stitch designs were referred to as 'Span[i]che stiche'. This name was adopted by the English too, who also called it 'trew [true] stitch', because the patterns were identical on the front and back of the embroidery . Randalle Holme referred to double running stitch in his work, The Academy of Armoury, published in 1688, as 'Spanish stitch, true on both sides'.

As the years passed, Spanish stitch became known as Holbein stitch. This name derived from the precise paintings by artist Hans Holbein of courtiers, whose collars, cuffs and bodices were embroidered with double running stitch.

Historic 'Brown work' from Toledo

Historic Lagartera Mats

PREPARING YOUR FABRIC

Always overcast your fabric before commencing your piece to prevent fraying. When using even-weave fabric, avoid overcasting in a straight line. If the fabric is inadvertently caught the whole group of overcast threads can be pulled off, thereby damaging the fabric edge.

Do not use adhesive tapes as an edging for embroidery pieces because the glue in these is almost impossible to remove and attracts a lot of dirt.

Leave a margin of 10 cm (4 inches) from each edge of the design. This allows sufficient fabric for framing or working a hem. If you prefer a wide hem, you will need to adjust this measurement.

Mark the vertical and the horizontal centre of your design with a light-coloured tacking thread. Avoid using dark-coloured thread as the colour may 'bleed', causing permanent discolouration of your work.

Avoid using washable or fading pens, biro or felt tip markers to mark a design. Washable pen ink may look like it has washed away but can suddenly reappear and it is permanent when it does. It is wise not to take the chance.

Use a small brass safety pin to mark the top and front of your work. Place the pin so that it does not interfere with your working area.

The linen count is:
    11 threads to the cm (28 threads to the inch)
    13 threads to the cm (32 threads to the inch).

The larger the count, the smaller the end result.

STARTING WORK

To knot or not to knot, when starting a new thread? If in doubt, don't. It is preferable to use a back stitch, or you can use a waste knot.

Waste knot

Make a knot in the end of the thread and take the needle through from the front of the fabric approximately 8 cm (3 inches) from where you plan to begin your work. Bring the needle up to the front ready to start the stitching. You will have a knot on the front and a long thread on the back of the fabric.

After completing about five stitches, lift the knot and cut. Then, using a spare needle and working on the back of your fabric, weave the end through three stitches in the same direction as you have been working – that is, horizontally or vertically – and back through two stitches, splitting the end thread on the return. This will lock the thread.

Do not leave a waste knot sitting on the
top of the fabric as it will leave a spot on the face of the work.
Finish it off as soon as possible.

When you need to finish off a thread, take it through to the back of your work and weave the end through three stitches and continue as outlined in the above paragraph.

Do not carry thread across the back
of your work from one satin stitch block to another.
Complete each block as you go.

LAGARTERA STITCHES

Satin stitch blocks

Satin stitch blocks are an important feature of Lagartera, providing colour, interest and change in texture.

Traditionally in a single design, the stitches in all motifs are worked in the same direction, either vertically or horizontally.

The number of strands used in the needle when working the satin stitch depends on the count of the linen. It is essential that the fabric be completely covered by the threads. More strands will be required as the linen count decreases.

The long satin stitches are brought up in a space and carried along the valley between the same parallel threads. Once the thread has passed over the required number of fabric threads it is taken down in the appropriate space. The stitches can be worked from the left or the right and vertically or horizontally. They are worked in the grooves of the linen. The number of fabric threads worked over in both directions is determined by the design you have chosen.

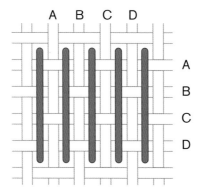

FIG. 1 *Five satin stitches equals four fabric threads enclosed.*

With certain designs (for example, the alphabet sampler on page 30), some satin stitches would be too long if they were all worked in the same direction. In such instances, you need to change direction so that no fabric threads show. The first stitch in the new direction shares the same valley as the previous block (see Fig. 2).

 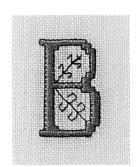  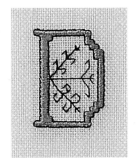

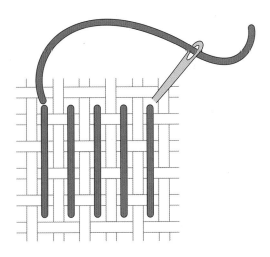

FIG. 2 *Changing direction.*

Antique hem stitch

Begin 5 cm (2 inches) from a corner and work along the grain of the fabric.

With the hem towards you, bring the thread under the fold with three running stitches and a backstitch to lock the thread.

Working from left to right, bring the thread out one fabric thread into the hem. Place the needle from right to left under three fabric threads, and then pull the thread through.

To complete the stitch, take the needle under the hem and out one fabric thread into the hem, three fabric threads from the last stitch in the hem.

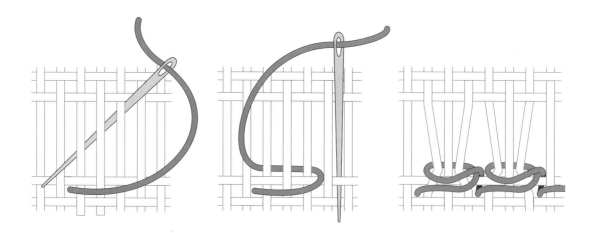

Back stitch

Back stitch is worked from right to left. Work over 2 fabric threads.

Bring the needle out at A, down at B & out again at C, 4 fabric threads to the left of B. Go back in at D (sharing the same hole as A) & out again at E.

Continue.

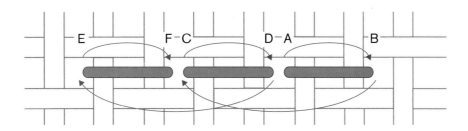

Double running stitch

This stitch is worked in two passes (or journeys). In the first pass, work every other stitch following your design. On the return pass, work the in-between stitches. The back and front of your work should look the same.

To achieve a straight line in double running stitch, your needle should come up below the previous stitch (sharing the same hole) on the return journey and down above the next stitch (also sharing the same hole). This must be done consistently.

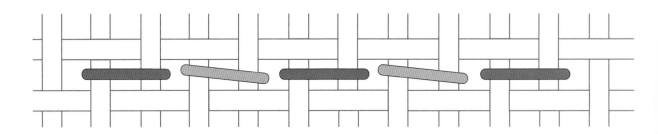

Four- sided stitch

Work over 2 fabric threads horizontally & vertically.

To start bring thread out at A, in at B out at C & in again at D.

Stitch as per the sequence shown in the diagram.

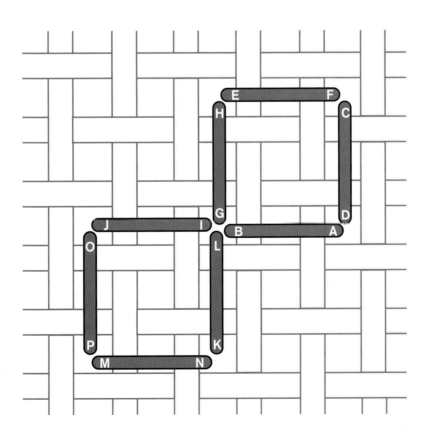

Nun stitch

Work over two fabric threads.

Work 2 horizontal back stitches to share the same holes.

Work 2 vertical back stitches as above sharing the right hand hole.

Work 2 more horizontal back stitches to share the lower right hand hole.

At a turn ensure the fifth diagram is followed to avoid a diagonal stitch appearing on the back of the work.

The fabric is cut away on the open side of the nun stitch. Pull out the appropriate fabric thread if necessary to ensure an accurate cutting line.

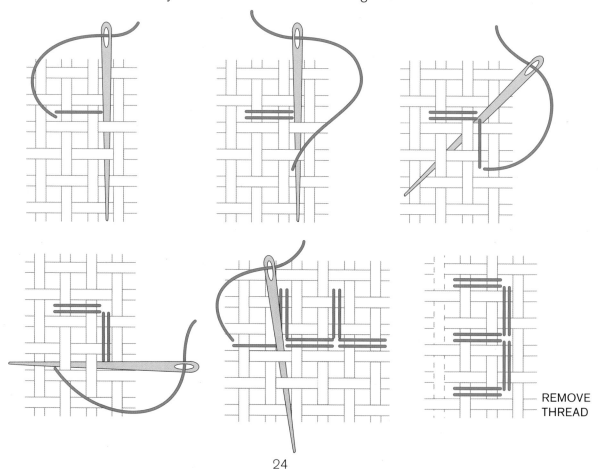

REMOVE
THREAD

Palestrina knot

Work over 4 fabric threads horizontally & 2 fabric threads vertically.

Bring needle out at A, insert at B, & re-emerge at C.

Work over & under the bar (not through the fabric).

Work over the bar again with the thread lying under the needle, & tension to form the knot.

Insert the needle 2 threads to the right of B & bring it out 2 threads diagonally below to be in line with B. This creates the next bar.

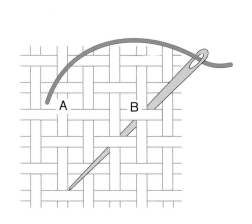

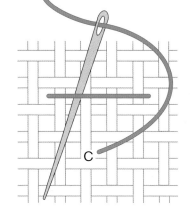

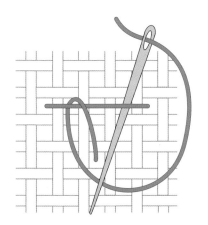

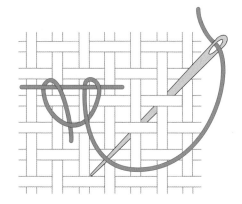

Buttonhole loop and bar

Use two strands of stranded thread to form the loop for the needle case and the bars for the small bag.

Anchor the thread on the left-hand side of the loop (or bar) with two tiny back stitches. *Form a loop large enough for the button (or cords) to pass through. (Bars for carrying cords can be almost flat against the fabric.) Take the thread back under the fabric (use the fold for the button loop) to the left-hand side. Repeat from *. Work the buttonhole stitch from left to right over these threads. The threads of the bar should not be visible, but do not overfill because the bar will twist. Fasten off neatly and firmly.

Helpful Hints

Working with thread

In most instances the length of thread should be no longer than 50 cm (20 inches), or about the distance between a thread held between your thumb and forefinger and your elbow Long thread tends to wear and this will ultimately show in your work. With Perle thread, constantly drawing it through fabric tends to cause friction, which warms the thread, causing it to become dull. Using a long thread will exacerbate this problem.

Most threads produce smoother and more even work if threaded so that the twist appears to run down from the needle. You should stitch with the twist not against it. Test the yarn after cutting by passing it lightly between the tip of the forefinger and the thumb, first from one end and then from the other. It is a good idea to close your eyes while doing this. The 'drag' will be greater in one direction than the other. Thread the needle in the direction of least 'drag'.

When preparing stranded threads, cut a piece no more than 50 cm (20 inches) in length just past a fold in the thread. This 'hook' will remind you which is the waste knot end. Divide the threads by holding the six strands between the thumb and forefinger and pulling upwards on one strand at a time, before placing the required number together again. This will provide better coverage.

To prevent marks on the fabric when removing thread, carefully snip the thread every 2 cms (¾ inch) or so. Then, using tweezers, pull each little piece of thread out quickly. Pulling quickly seems to prevent the unwanted thread leaving a shadow on the fabric.

Using a frame

Using a frame is optional. If using a round frame, cover the inner ring with cotton tape, as this helps to keep the fabric taut. Simply bind the ring with tape, turn the cut end under and stitch to secure.

Storing work

To store your work- in-progress or completed piece,roll onto a cardboard cylinder covered with light-coloured fabric or acid-free tissue paper to avoid making creases that can't be removed. The rolls from cling film or foil are ideal for this. Always roll your embroidery with the embroidered side facing outwards.

If unfinished pieces are to be stored for some time, place the rolled piece in a cotton fabric bag or roll it in another layer of cotton fabric to protect from dust.

Small pieces can be laid flat with acid- free tissue in between.

Cleaning and finishing

Do not spray your embroidery with starch (moths just love starch), fabric protector or similar products. Chemicals tend to rot and discolour fabric over time.

Never use a product containing any form of bleach on your embroidery. Chlorine-based products are much too harsh for delicate work.

Wash embroidery gently and quickly, using pure soap flakes. Rinse thoroughly, at least twice, in demineralised water, and dry your embroidery quickly to prevent colours running.

To remove excess moisture, roll your embroidery in a white towel and squeeze gently. Remove the embroidery and press until dry or use a hairdryer to blow it dry. If pressing dry, place the piece face down on a clean white sheet laid over a blanket. Place a white pressing cloth over the top and press until dry.

LAGARTERA PROJECTS

This section contains 27 designs. The instructions for some show how they can be used on a number of different items. Some designs can also be adapted to suit your requirements by adding or deleting design elements, and the large motifs can be used as single designs.

Before starting work, read the general instructions at the beginning of the book. You may also need to refer to the instructions at the end of the book to help you in finishing your project.

The degree of difficulty for these projects is indicated by:

Beginner	✂
Intermediate	✂ ✂
Experienced	✂ ✂ ✂

Alphabet Sampler

Requirements

- Permin Danish even-weave linen (Sandstone), 28 count, 35.5 x 45.5 cm (14 x 18 inches)
- Tapestry needle no. 24 or 26
- DMC stranded cotton: black (310), light mahogany (3776), medium avocado green (937), and medium antique blue (931)
- Light-coloured tacking thread

Design

The embroidered area measures 20 x 30.5 cms (8 x 12 inches).

Stitches

Satin and double running stitch

Preparation

1. Refer to the general instructions before commencing.
2. Note that each square on the chart equals two fabric threads.
3. Use a light- coloured thread to mark the top and the bottom of each row of letters with a running stitch over four fabric threads
4. Three strands of cotton are used for the satin stitch and one strand of black for the double running outline.

Method of working

1. Work each letter from the bottom. The marking lines make it easier to count the next starting point and also serve as a check that the letters have been worked correctly.
2. The alphabet is worked in satin stitch, using three strands of cotton. The horizontal lines are worked in a vertical direction and the vertical lines are worked in a the horizontal direction. When changing direction, it is essential to follow the instructions on page 18 (see also Fig. 2).
3. Using one strand of black cotton, outline the letters in double running stitch over two fabric threads. At the corners it may be necessary to work over three fabric threads.

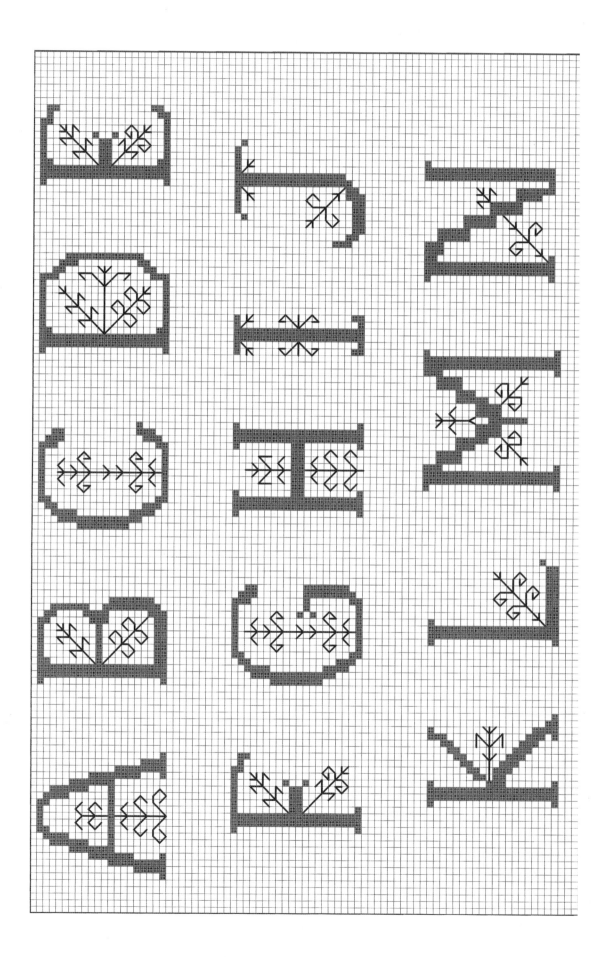

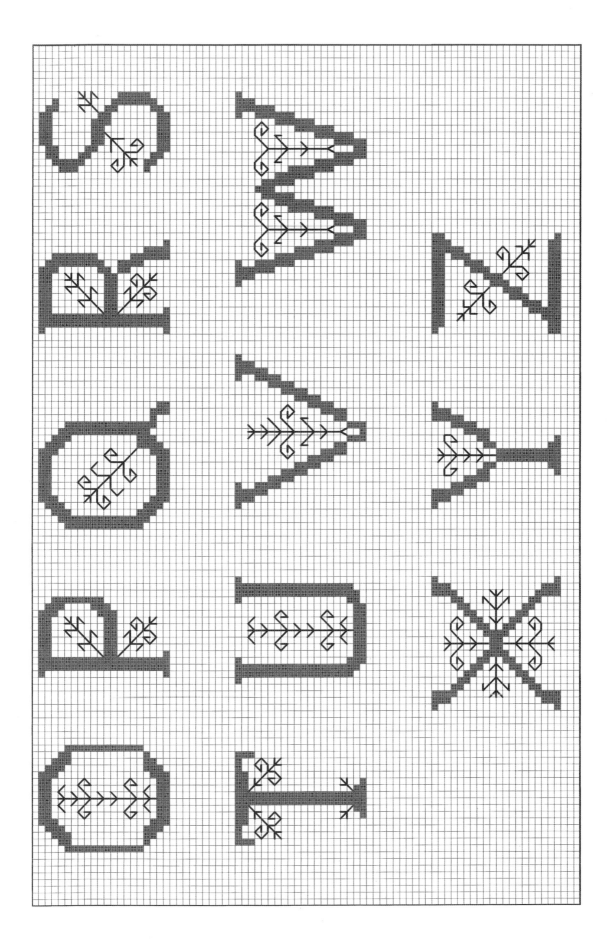

English Rose Table Runner

Requirements

- Permin Danish even-weave linen (English Rose), 28 count, 80 x 35 cms (31 1/2 x 13 3/4 inches)
- Tapestry needle no. 24 or 26
- Crewel needle no. 7
- DMC stranded cotton: medium antique violet (3041), dark pine green (3362) and straw (3821).
- Tapestry Needles No.24 or No.26, and a No.7 crewel needle.
- Medium tone tacking thread.

Design

The embroidered area measures 62 x 19 cms (24 1/2 x 7 1/2 inches).

Stitches

Satin stitch blocks, double running, back, antique hem and slip stitch

Preparation

1. Refer to the general instructions before commencing.
2. Note that each square on the chart equals two fabric threads.
3. Mark the centres over four fabric threads. You may like to tack extra reference lines along the long edges. These will assist in keeping your count accurate.
4. All double running is worked with one strand of thread and the satin stitch is worked with two strands.

By just stitching the barest outline in the first round of
a larger piece you will reduce the amount of unpicking needed
if your counting is not accurate.

Method of working

1. Start with a waste knot.

2. Work over two fabric threads using double running stitch and one strand of dark pine green (3362). Start stitching on a long side, six fabric threads to the right of the tacked centre line, and stitch the inside line of the medium diamond, the straight line, the inside line of the large diamond, the straight line, and so on. When you come to the corner just stitch the inside edge of the large diamond. Plan to start and finish your thread within a diamond.

3. On the return journey, work all the embellishments and the counted satin stitch diamonds. Stitch the diamonds according to the chart, using two strands of medium antique violet (3041) for the large and small diamonds and two strands of straw (3821) for the medium diamonds. The satin stitch starts one fabric thread in and one fabric thread down from the point of the diamond. The double running stitch and the satin stitch will share alternate holes except at these corners. Wherever possible, work the satin stitch before the double running stitch to avoid splitting the running stitch, which occurs more often when coming up through the fabric.

Your stitching must join accurately when you have completed the first round.

Hem

1. Refer to the instructions on mitring a corner and folding a hem on page 82.

2. On all four sides, count out 36 fabric threads from the last stitch of a large motif and withdraw the 37th thread. Then remove the 38th thread and weave it back at the corners into the space left from removing the 37th thread.

3. Count out ten10 fabric threads on all four sides and, starting in a corner, work back stitch over four fabric threads around the runner using two strands of medium antique violet (3041). This is the outside edge of the runner. The back stitch will give a very definite fold line.

4. Count out a further eight fabric threads and mark with a tacking thread all the way round. Count out a further six fabric threads and trim away the excess fabric.

5. Using one strand of medium antique violet (3041), work antique hem stitch over four fabric threads.

6. Remove all tacking threads and press.

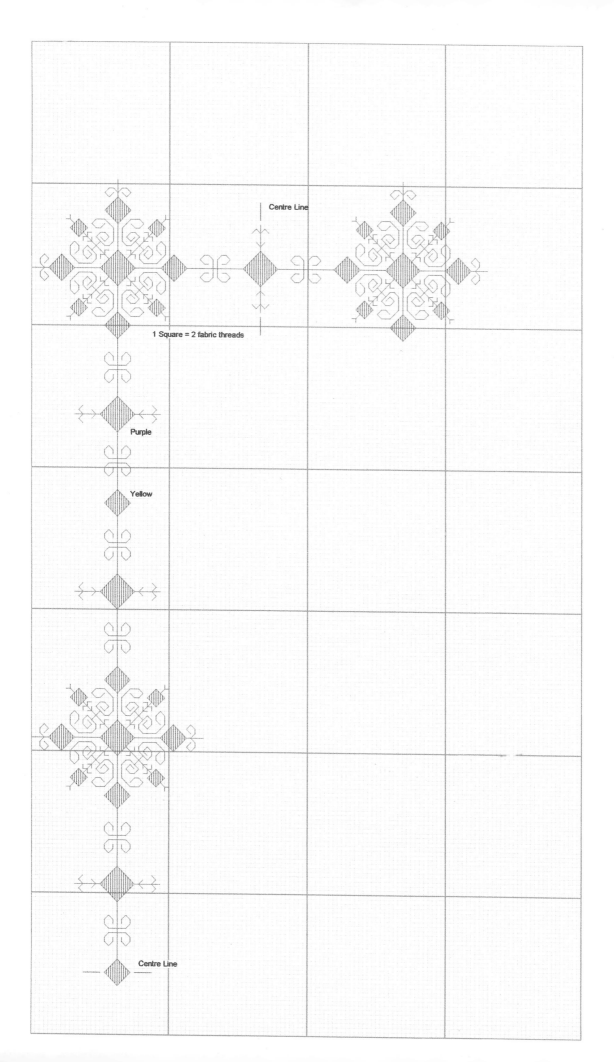

Centre Line

1 Square = 2 fabric threads

Purple

Yellow

Centre Line

The design can be adapted to suit your requirements by
adding or deleting design elements.
The large motif can be used as a single motif.

Chatelaine, Pin Cushion, Scissor Fob, Needle Case and Small Bag

Requirements

- Permin Danish even-weave linen (Antique Tan), 28 count, 140 x 30 cms (55 x 12 inches)
- Tapestry needle no. 24 or 26
- Crewel needle no. 7
- DMC stranded cotton: ultra dark beaver grey (844)), two skeins medium shell pink (3722), straw (3821), dark pine green (3362).
- Medium tone tacking thread
- Iron-on interfacing for needle case, 20 x 12 cm (8 x 4¾ inches)
- Lining fabric for needle case and bag, 40 x 15 cms (15¾ x 6 inches)
- Plain cotton fabric for pin cushion inner, 30 x 15 cm (12 x 6 inches)
- Thin pellon, two pieces, 140 x 6 cm (55 x 2½ inches) and 17 x 9 cm (6¾ x 3½ inches)
- Small quantity fibre filling for pin cushion and scissor fob
- Baby flannel for needle case leaves, 18 x 7 cm (7 x 2¾ inches).
- One small rounded button with a shank to close needle case.
- One metal washer or old coin for scissor fob.

Fabric requirements

Label each piece to avoid confusion later..

Chatelaine strap: cut one piece, 140 x 13.5 cm wide (55 x 5¼ inches).

Pin cushion: cut two pieces, each 13 x 11 cm (5 x 4¼ inches)

Scissor fob: cut two pieces, each 6.5 x 6.5 cm (2½ x 2½ inches).

Needle case: cut one piece, 20 x 13 cm (8 x 5 inches).

Small bag: cut one piece, 15 x 15 cm (6 x 6 inches).

Stitches

Double running, counted satin, palestrina knot, slip stitch

Preparation

Mark the centres over three fabric threads.

Chatelaine

Method of working

1. Refer to the general instructions.
2. Tack a line 9 cm (3½ inches) from the bottom of the chatelaine strap.
3. Start stitching on this line six fabric threads to the left of your marked vertical centre line – at the arrow.
4. Use a single strand of ultra dark beaver grey (844) and work over three fabric threads. First work the bare outline of the design in double running stitch. When you have reached the top of the design and are ready for the return journey, use two strands of thread and work all the flower centres in straw (3821) and the leaves in dark pine green (3362). Note: To avoid very long stitches, the leaves are worked in bands of satin stitch over three fabric threads.
5. Work the flower petals with two strands of medium shell pink (3722) as you come to them and complete the double running outline and all the embellishments.
6. Repeat the design on the other end of the strap as a mirror image.
7. Work two single motifs each side of the centre back, with the top petal 15 fabric threads from the centre back. Work these as a mirror image also.

Chatelaine edge

Tack a line, 30 fabric threads each side of the centre, along the long edges. This will be the fold line. Starting 2.5 cm (1 inch) from the bottom of the strap and using three strands of medium shell pink (3722), work palestrina knot over four fabric threads and work one fabric thread either side of the tacked fold line.

If desired, the strap may be edged with a twisted cord, which is stitched on after the strap has been constructed.

Construction of the strap

Remove the lengthways tacking threads. Leave the crossways tacking threads as they will assist in the final construction.

Trim pellon marginally smaller than the width of the chatelaine strap between the rows of palestrina knot. (Join the pellon if necessary.). Lay the pellon on the inside of the strap, 2.5 cm (1 inch) from the bottom on each side. Fold over 2.5 cm (1 inch) of linen on each bottom edge. Then fold along one long stitched edge to partially enclose the pellon and tack in place. Adjust the length of the pellon if necessary. Turn under approximately 1 cm (3/8 inch) along the other long side, fold and tack into place to fully enclose the pellon, aligning the crossways tacking lines. Slip stitch, using matching thread, along the length of the chatelaine strap. Remove all tacking lines and press.

Assembling the chatelaine

Slip the loop of the pin cushion on to one side of the strap and the loops of the needle case and the small bag on to the other. (See instructions for these items on the following pages.) Turn up 3 cm (1 1/4 inches) on each end to keep the loops in place and slip stitch these ends to the inside of the strap. Other pieces can be added to the chatelaine as required.

To make the outline stand out more clearly,
the satin stitch is worked inside the outline, i.e. instead of
the usual seven satin stitches across five fabric threads
you will work 5 stitches across four fabric threads.

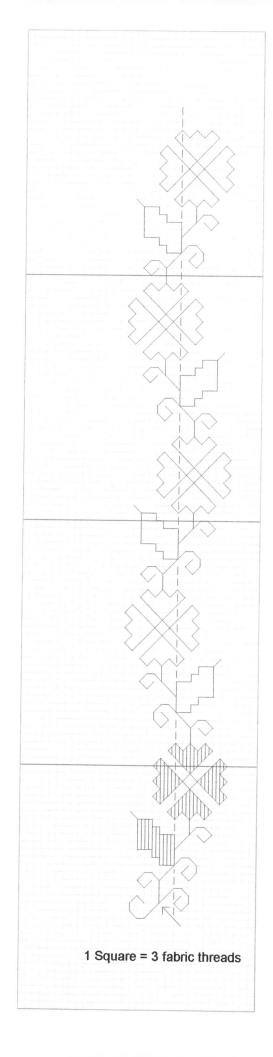

1 Square = 3 fabric threads

Pin Cushion

With single motif work, the centre of the flower is placed on the vertical centre of the fabric (see instructions on page 64). Tack the outside boundaries on both pieces of the fabric, starting at the centre line on the long side, 45 fabric threads from the centre. Tack up 60, across 90, down 120, across 90 and up 60 fabric threads.

Following the instructions for the chatelaine strap, work the bottom motif on the chart on to the pin cushion. Press the embroidery.

Starting at the bottom right-hand corner, make up the pin cushion following the instructions on page 83.

Then make 70 cm (27½ inches) of twisted cord (see instructions on page 85) from six lengths of medium shell pink (3722).

Before stitching the twisted cord to the pin cushion, attach 15 cm (6 inches) of the cord to the top of the pin cushion, at the corner, to allow it to hang from the chatelaine strap.

Scissor Fob

Tack the outside boundaries over three fabric threads on both pieces of fabric, 48 x 48 fabric threads.

Work the flower petals only in the centre of one piece, following the instructions given for the chatelaine strap.

Make up the scissor fob with the cord and the tassel on opposite corners (refer to the instructions of page 84). You will need approximately 50 cm (20 inches) of twisted cord made from four lengths of medium shell pink (3722) Use one strand of 3722 to wrap the head of the tassel.

Needle Case

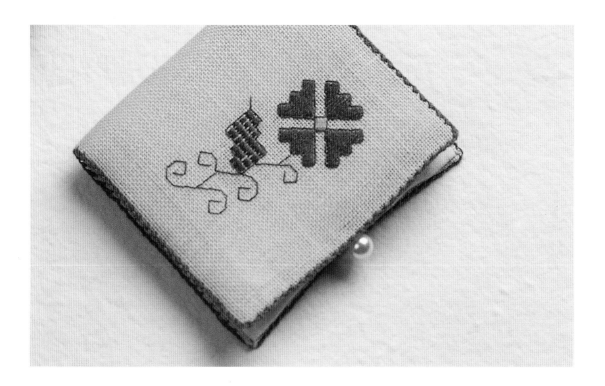

Outer case

Leave approximately 1 cm (3/8 inch) seam allowance. Tack mark the needle case boundary over four fabric threads, 188 fabric threads wide by 104 fabric threads deep. Tack two extra lines − 84 fabric threads from each short edge. The 20 fabric threads between these lines is the spine. Mark the centre lines on the front (right-hand side section) and work a flower, following the instructions given for the chatelaine strap. Then embroider the bottom motif on the chart on the front. Remove the long centre tacking line.

Using three strands of medium shell pink (3722), work palestrina knot (as for the chatelaine strap) around the outside edge of the needle case.

Stitch simple mitred corners, following the instructions on page 83. Cut pellon marginally smaller than the inside of the needle case. Fold over the seam allowances along the stitched line and tack into place over the pellon.

Inner case

Cut out a piece of interfacing, 9 x 16.5 cm (3½ x 6½ inches), and iron on to a piece of lining fabric, 12 x 20 cm (4¾ x 8 inches). Fold the edge of the lining fabric under and press. The lining fabric should fit just inside the outer case. Adjust if necessary.

Cut the flannel into two pieces, each 9 x 16.5 cm (3½ x 6½ inches), and trim to 8 x 16 cm (3 x 6¼ inches) with pinking shears. Align to the centre of the lining fabric and attach to the flannel down the centre.

Beginning at the centre bottom, stitch the lining to the soft outer cover using a matching sewing thread and slip stitch just inside the palestrina knot edge.

Make a twisted cord, 25 cm (10 inches) long, by using four strands of medium shell pink (3722), 80 cm (31½ inches) long. Follow the instructions on page 85. Insert the cord at the centre top to form a loop and attach firmly. This loop will be used to attach the needle case to the chatelaine.

To close the needle case, make a small buttonhole loop just inside the front edge of the needle case. Attach the small button to the back edge. Check that the button will slip through the loop.

Small Bag

Suitable for storing your thimble, tape measure and other small sewing tools, this bag is 144 x 144 fabric threads plus seam allowances.

Tack mark the outside boundaries. Then fold the fabric in half lengthways and tack mark the vertical centre of one half over three fabric threads.

Work the bottom motif from the chart starting at the arrow, 12 fabric threads from the bottom boundary, and centring the middle peak of the top flower petals on the vertical centre.

Work one row of palestrina knot 27 fabric threads from the top boundary. This will be the fold line. From the right side, using matching thread, slip stitch the side and the bottom seams together very neatly.

Cut out a piece of lining, approximately 15 x 11 cm (6 x 4¼ inches). Measure your bag width to determine the seam allowance and allow a little extra. Sew the long sides of the lining together. With the right sides together, sew the lining top to the bag top. Adjust the length of the lining to fit the bag and close the bottom seam. Turn the lining inside the bag along the fold line. Remove all the tacking threads and press.

To carry the closing cords, work two button hole bars on each side of the bag (four in all), 3 cm (1¼ inches) from the top of the bag. You can also work a bar at the centre front and back. You will need two cords, each 30 cm (12 inches), to close the bag.

Four lengths of stranded thread, 2.5 metres (8 feet) long, made into a twisted cord should be sufficient to make two cords (see instructions on page 85). Tie a knot in the cords and fluff out the ends. NOTE: 2.5 M IS approx. 8 FT

If you wish to attach the bag to your chatelaine you will need extra cord.

Pin Cushion

Requirements

- Permin Danish Linen (Ecru), 28 count, 15 x 15 cm (6 x 6 inches)
- Tapestry needle no. 24
- DMC stranded cotton: black (310) for running stitch, and red (321) and emerald green (699) for satin stitch
- Plain cotton material for inner cushion 16 x 32 cm (6 ¼ x 12½ inches)
- Small quantity of fibre filling.
- Twisted cord, purchased or hand made

Design

1. The embroidered area is measures 108 x 108 fabric threads. Allow 2 cm (¾ inch) on each side of the design so that it does not appear to 'fall off' when the pin cushion is filled.
2. The pin cushion is 144 x 144 fabric threads plus seam allowances.
3. Use three strands of cotton for satin stitch and one strand for double running stitch.

Stitches

Double running, counted satin and slip stitch

Preparation

1. Mark the centre lines over four fabric threads (see instructions on page 83). If you wish, mark the top of your fabric.
2. Tack the outside boundaries on both pieces of the fabric by counting out 72 fabric threads along one centre line. Tack up 72, across 144, down 144, across 144 and up 72 fabric threads. These tacking lines will also help with your slip stitch.

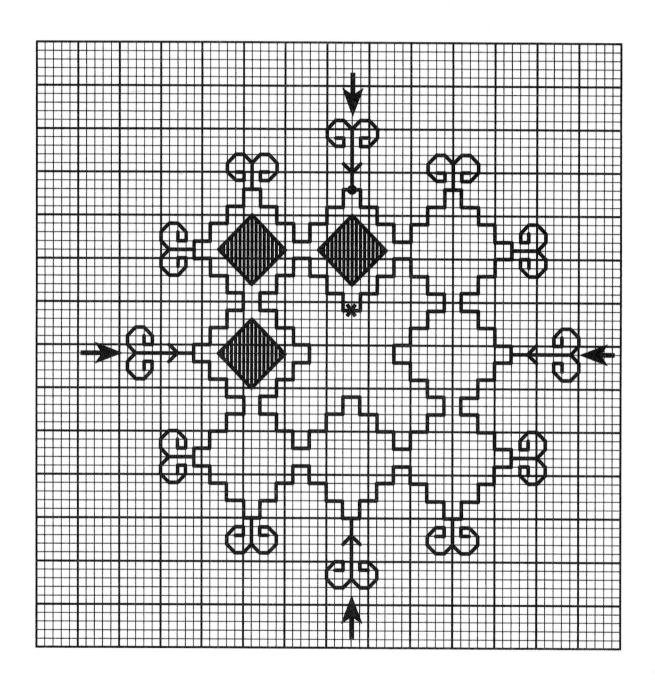

Method of working

1. Start inner double running border at x – ten fabric threads from the centre. Work as per stitch diagram, each stitch to be worked over two fabric threads.

2. Start outer double running border at . – 38 fabric threads from the centre. Stitch as above, working branches on the return journey.

3. Note: All satin stitch diamonds are stitched in the same direction. Stitch according to the chart. The satin stitch starts one fabric thread below the centre of each diamond and seven fabric threads in from the double running border. This allows the double running outline to start directly at the centre line, six fabric threads in from the border, thus forming perfect diamonds.

4. Border the satin stitch diamonds in double running stitch. The double running shares the same holes as the satin stitch except in the corner as explained in 3.

Finishing

Make up the pin cushion . If you wish, you can make the cord by following the instructions on page 85.

Alternate colour suggestions

1. Permin Danish Linen (Ecru), 28 count
    DMC stranded cotton: black (310) for double running stitch, and dark lemon (444) and dark royal blue (796) for satin stitch

2. Permin Danish Linen (Ecru), 28 count
    DMC stranded cotton: dark pewter grey (413) for double running, and medium dark antique mauve (315) and dark blue-green (501) for satin stitch

3. Permin Danish Linen (Wild Raspberry), 28 count
    DMC stranded cotton: Ecru for double running and satin stitch

4. Permin Danish Linen (Antique Rose), 28 count
    DMC stranded cotton: winter white (3865) for double running and satin stitch

5. Permin Danish Linen (Ecru), 28 count
    DMC stranded cotton: slate grey (413) for double running, and sage green (501) and deep pink (315) for satin stitch

Bookmark

The bookmark design is an adaptation of the pin cushion design. Extra diamonds have been added along one side, with embellishments on each end.

Requirements
- Even-weave linen, 28 count, 26.5 x 9.5 cm (10½ x 3¾ inches)
- Tapestry needle no. 24 or 26
- DMC stranded cotton (see suggestions below)

Stitches
Double running, counted satin and nun stitch.

Preparation
Mark the centres over four fabric threads.

Method of working
1. Follow the chart and instructions for the pin cushion, adding one extra diamond top and bottom.
2. Start and finish with the same colour thread.
3. With matching or contrasting stranded thread, work nun stitch around the outside, 1 cm (³⁄8 inch) from the centre on the long sides and 1.5 cm (⁵⁄8 inch) above the embellishments on each end. Withdraw one thread outside the nun stitch on the long sides. Trim away the excess fabric on the long sides and fringe the narrow ends.

Colour suggestions
1. Permin Danish Linen (Ecru), 28 count DMC stranded cotton: dark pewter grey (413) for double running, and medium dark antique mauve (315) and dark blue-green (501) for satin stitch
2. Permin Danish Linen (Ecru), 28 count DMC stranded cotton: very dark brown-grey (3021) for double running, and dark antique blue (930) and very dark old gold (3829) for satin stitch
3. Coloured linen, 28 count DMC stranded cotton: Ecru or winter white (3865) for double running and satin stitch

58

Scissor Fob

The scissor fob design is a single diamond with embellishments on all four sides.

Requirements

- Fabric requirements depend on the thread count of the linen (a completed scissor fob is 60 x 60 fabric threads). Add an extra 1.5 cm ($^5/_8$ inch) seam allowance.
- Tapestry needle no. 24 or 26
- DMC stranded cotton (colours of your choice).
- Narrow strip of fine pellon.
- One metal washer or old coin.
- Twisted cord, purchased or hand made

Stitches

Double running and counted satin stitch

Preparation

Mark the centres over four fabric threads (see instructions on page 83).

Method of working

1. Following the chart, work a single motif and the embellishments.
2. Make up the scissor fob following the instructions on page 84.

Box Top

Requirements

- Even-weave linen, 28 count, 34.5 x 26.5 cm (13½ x 10½ inches)
- Tapestry needle no. 24 or 26
- DMC stranded cotton: very dark pewter grey (3799), very dark peacock blue (3765), dark burnt orange (900)
- Medium tone tacking thread

Design

1. The embroidered area measures 19 x 11.5 cm (7½ x 4½ inches)
2. Note that each square on the chart equals two fabric threads

Stitches

Double running, four-sided and satin stitch.

Preparation

Mark the centre and work over two fabric threads.

Method of working

1. Work the double running and four-sided stitches with one strand of cotton and all satin stitches with two strands of cotton.

2. Referring to the chart and the photograph to check colour placement, start at the centre point and stitch work all the double running and four- sided stitching in very dark pewter grey (3799). Then fill in the shapes on the outer edges with satin stitch, using very dark peacock blue cotton (3765), and all the inner shapes with dark burnt orange (900).

Table Mat

The design for the table mat was adapted from the design of the cuff on the costume worn by Jane Seymour in Hans Holbein's 1537 portrait.

It is worked with one strand of silk in double running stitch over two fabric threads.

This piece was worked on Wild Raspberry 32 count Permin Danish Linen, using one skein (8 metres – 26 feet) of Au-ver-a-Soie (Soie d'Alger) Crème Silk.

Motif Sampler

Requirements

- White even-weave fabric, 26 count, 30 x 30 cm (12 x 12 inches)
- Tapestry needle no. 24
- One ball DMC No. 12 perle cotton: black
- One skein DMC metallic thread: gold (5282)
- One reel Gutermann silk sewing thread: black
- Sewing thread: white and a contrasting pale shade (see instructions on 'Preparing your fabric')
- Round hoop, 20 cm (8 inches) (optional) (see instructions on 'Using a frame')

Design

The embroidered area measures 12 x 12 cm (4¾ x 4¾ inches) square.

Stitches

Double running stitch.

Preparation

1. Refer to the general instructions before commencing.
2. Note that each square on the chart equals two fabric threads.

Method of working

1. Start at arrow A to work the first line. The motif areas will be created as you stitch the return journey.
2. Starting at the X follow the chart to complete the other two lines.
3. Work all of motif 1 in no. 12 perle cotton (black), starting at the arrow. Work the cross in the centre in gold (5282) thread.
4. Work motifs 2 and 3 in no. 12 perle cotton (black). An arrow shows the starting point for each motif. Work the separate crosses in the gold thread.
5. First work all the outlines for motifs 4, 5, 6 and 7 in no. 12 perle cotton (black)first. An arrow shows the starting point for each motif. Then work the centre pattern for each in the silk thread and the separate crosses in gold (5282).

6. Work motifs 8 and 9 in no. 12 perle cotton, starting at the arrow in each case. Then work the centre in gold.

7. Work the border, by following the chart and stitching a zigzag line. On the return journey stitch all the embellishments.

Finishing

Refer to the general instructions.

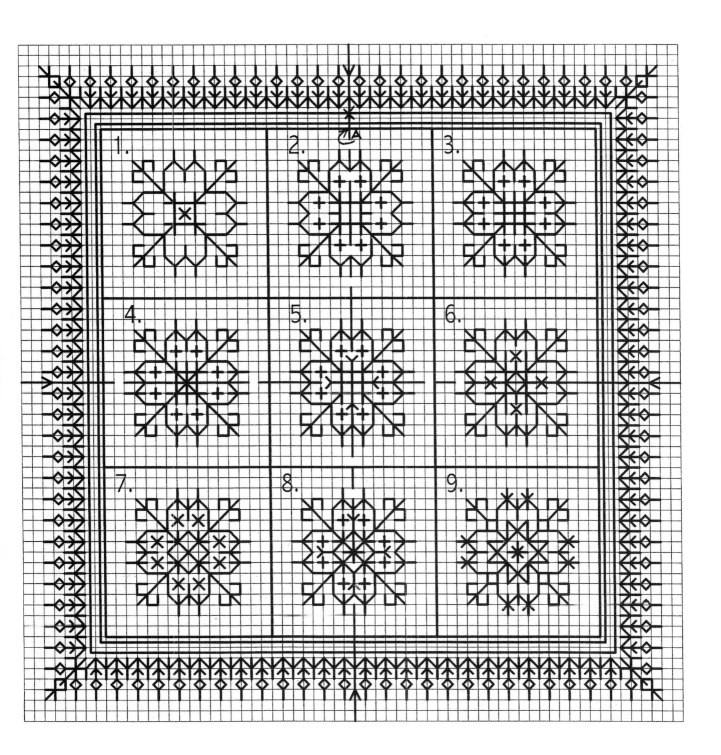

Pattern
Filling

Pattern
Filling

Pattern
Filling

Carnations

Requirements

- White even-weave fabric, 26 count, 30 x 30 cm (12 x 12 inches)
- Tapestry needle no. 24
- Two reels Gutermann top stitching thread: black
- Sewing thread: white and a contrasting pale shade
- Round hoop, 20 cm (8 inches) (optional)

Design

The embroidered area measures 15.5 x 15.5 cm (6 x 6 inches) square.

Stitches

Double running stitch.

Preparation

1. Refer to the general instructions before commencing work.
2. Note that each square on the chart equals two fabric threads.

Method of working

1. Begin your embroidery from the centre of the design.
2. Work all the central design first before adding the pattern filling on the chart.
3. Remove the tacking thread as you stitch.
4. For the pattern filling, complete all the double running squares first, then stitch the half cross in each square, before completing the cross on the return journey.
5. To work the border, begin by following the chart and stitching a zigzag line. On the return journey work all the embellishments.

   The single stitches below the border are stitched last.

Finishing

Refer to the general instructions.

Tile Designs

Requirements

- Aida fabric (Ecru), 14 count, 30 x 50 cm (12 x 20 inches)
- Tapestry needle no. 24
- Two reels Gutermann top stitching thread: navy blue (310).
- Sewing thread: ecru and a contrasting pale shade
- Round hoop, 20 cm (8 inches) (optional) (see instructions on 'Using a frame').

Design

The embroidered area measures 15 x 21 cm (6 x 8¼ inches).

Stitches

Double running stitch.

Preparation

1. Refer to the general instructions before commencing work.
2. Each square on the chart equals two fabric threads.

Method of working

1. Begin your embroidery from the centre of each tile.
   Remove the tacking thread as you stitch.
2. For the border, the arrows show the starting points.
   Following the chart, work two separate zigzag lines, stitching the
   embellishments on the return journey of the last line.

Finishing

Refer to the general instructions.

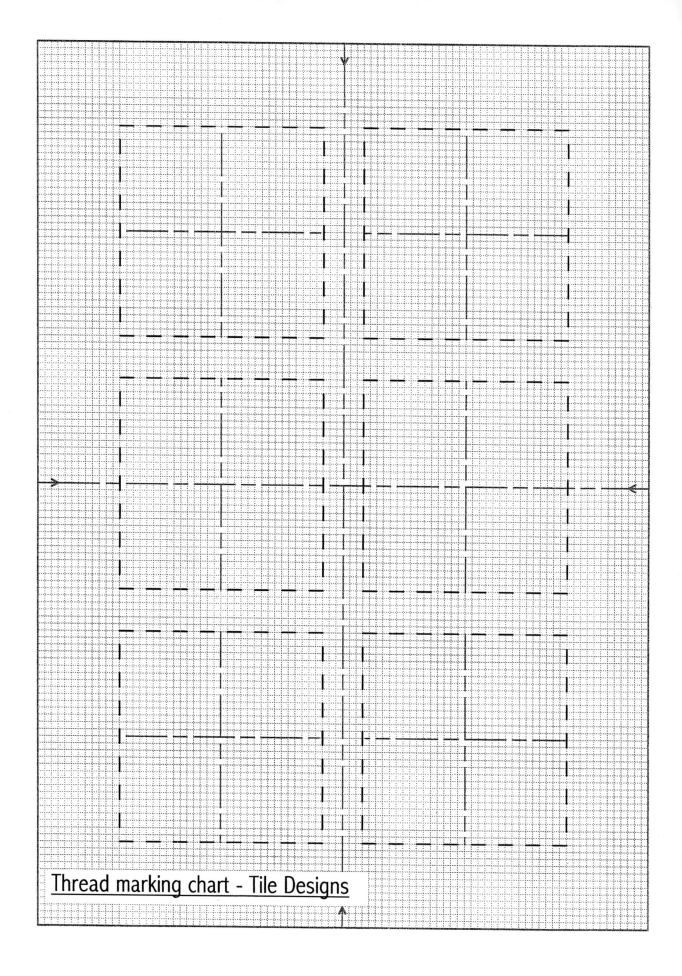

Thread marking chart - Tile Designs

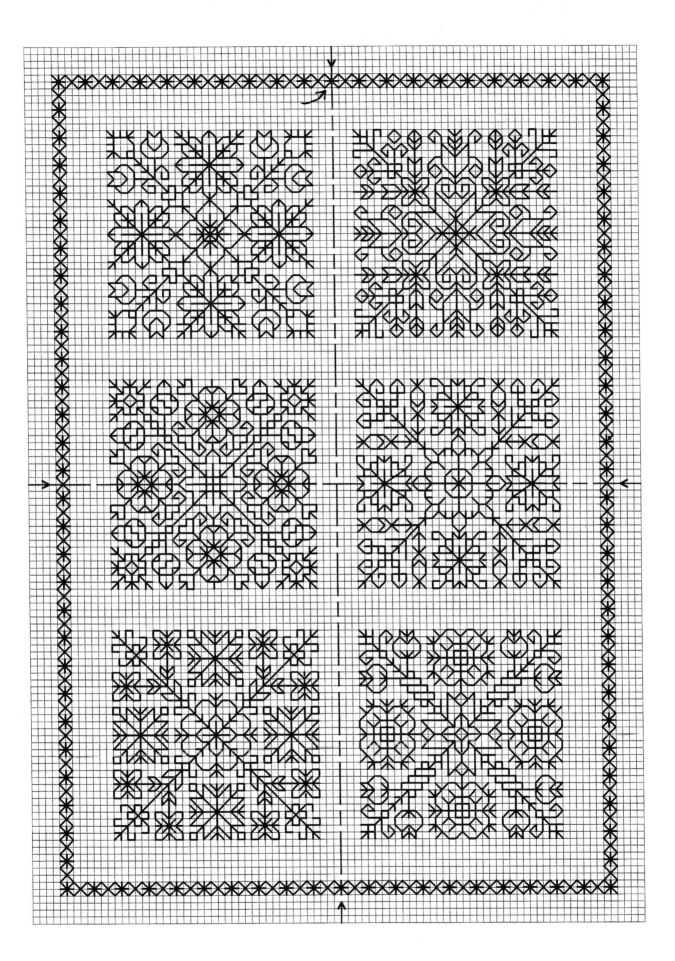

Novelty Designs, Borders and Edges

Requirements
- Lugana even-weave fabric
- Tapestry needles nos. 22 and 24
- DMC Perle thread no. 8: black (310), dark steel grey (414), tan (436), dark navy blue (823)
- DMC Perle thread no. 5: medium emerald green (911), very dark coral red (817), dark royal blue (796), medium yellow (743), very dark violet (550), medium blue (826), light shell pink (223)
- Embroidery hoop (optional)

Stitches
Satin and back stitch and French knot

Preparation
1. Refer to the general instructions before commencing.
2. Note that each square on the graph equals two fabric threads.

Method of working
1. For the balloon, sailboat, butterfly and ice-cream, work the satin stitch first.
2. For the train, bear and, elephant, satin stitch can be worked after the outline has been completed.
   Work a French knot for the elephant's eye.
3. For the borders and edges, each square on the graph equals two fabric threads.

Borders and Edges

Method of working

1. For the borders and edges, each square on the graph equals two fabric threads.

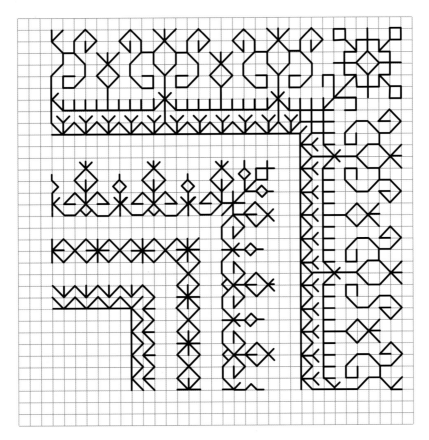

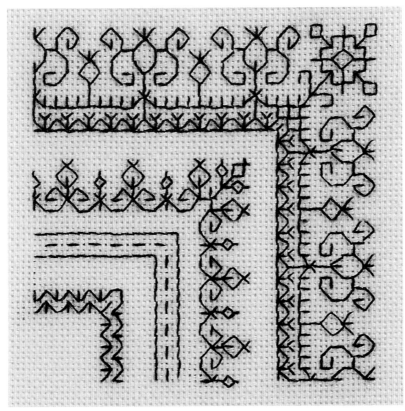

FINISHING

Folding a hem

Decide on the width of your hem and count the fabric threads. As an example, this number may be ten.

Mark the inside edge of the hem with a tacking line (or withdraw the threads as in the runner). Mark another tacking line the hem width (i.e. ten fabric threads) away from this line.

Count out ten minus two fabric threads (i.e. eight) and mark with a tacking line at the eighth thread. Count out a further ten minus four fabric threads (i.e. six) and trim away the excess fabric accurately.

You now have three rows of tacking, the outside one being no. 1, the middle one no. 2 and the inside one no. 3.

Line no. 2 can be worked with back stitch after tacking.

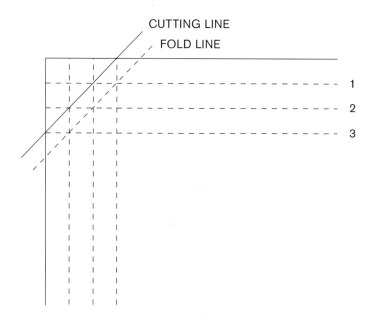

Fold the edge of the fabric to tacking line no. 2 on all four sides so that line no. 1 is on the fold. Once again, fold the fabric in, so that no. 1 is placed one fabric thread outside no. 3.

Press the four sides carefully. Do not move the iron back and forth. Lift it and place it down on the next area. Open up the fabric and press a fold across the corner.

Mitring a corner

To remove the excessive bulk in each of the corners of your work, remove some of the fabric by cutting the corner off where the tacking lines no. 1 and no. 2 intersect (see above). Press a fold across the corner. Re-fold the sides and corners to form mitred corners.

Slip stitch these corners, bringing the thread from the inside to the corner and stitching from the outer corner towards the inner corner.

Square corners: Leave a 'tail' when starting to stitch. This can then be gently pulled in to square off the corner and then fastened off.

Starting a pin cushion and scissor fob

When making a pin cushion or scissor fob with even-weave fabric, you need to first define their size with a tacking thread, and then allow approximately 1.5 cm (5/8 inch) seam allowance outside this boundary. Mark the centre in both directions with a tacking thread.

After you have worked the embroidery, press face down.

Finishing a pin cushion

Fold the corners of the pin cushion diagonally across the tacking lines. Fold in the edges to form simple mitred corners. Slip stitch the corners.

Align the tack-marked centres to maintain accuracy and slip stitch three sides using matching sewing thread.

Make an inner cushion from plain cotton fabric 5 mm (1/4 inch) larger on all four sides than the cushion outer. Fill firmly and close.
The inner cushion prevents the fibre filling from 'bleeding' through the outer fabric.

Insert the inner cushion and complete slip stitch, leaving a small opening to hide the ends of the twisted cord.

Attach the twisted cord with matching thread, stitching through the cord and easing it around the corners. This prevents the cord appearing to 'fall off'. Hide the ends of the cord in the opening and close up completely.

Tassels can be formed on the corners if you wish, but remember to allow extra twisted cord for the 'tails'.

Finishing a scissor fob

Join the pieces together as for the pin cushion.

Wrap the metal washer or old coin in the narrow strip of the fine pellon until well padded. Insert into the scissor fob and close up the opening. Theoretically, if your scissors fall, the weight of the washer/coin should prevent them from falling point downwards and being damaged.

Start attaching the twisted cord at a corner or centre bottom (depending on the design). Leave 3–4 cm (about 1 1/4 inches) of cord free before starting. Form a loop directly opposite the 'tail', for attaching the fob to the scissors, by twisting the cord around itself once before sewing it to the scissor fob. Make the loop large enough for the scissor fob to go through when attaching it to the scissors. Continue around to the 'tail', making another 'tail', and finish off firmly. Wrap the two 'tails' firmly together to form a small tassel. Trim and fluff out the tassel

Ease the cord around the corners to prevent it appearing to ' fall off'.

Making a twisted cord

To decide on the thickness for a twisted cord and the number of lengths of thread required, twist together a number of 30 cm (12 inch) lengths of thread (folded – not cut) and allow them to twist back on themselves. Add or remove strands to obtain the required thickness. Six lengths of unseparated stranded cotton make a generous cord for a pin cushion. Four lengths suit a scissor fob and ties for a small bag. The bigger the bag, the thicker the cord should be.

To determine the length of the threads, measure the circumference of the article, say 60 cm (24 inches). Multiply the 60 cm (24 inches) by 3 and add one-third of the circumference measurement (i.e. 60 x 3 = 180 + 20 = 200 cm, or approx. 80 inches). If you are making the cord for a scissor fob, don't forget to add the amount needed for the loop.

Make sure the cord is very firmly twisted
or it will soon look shabby.

BIBLIOGRAPHY

Barredo de Valenzuela, Fernando A. et al. *Artesania de Castilla la Mancha*.
de la edicion Centro de Promocion de la Artesania Mezquita de Tornerias, Junta de
Comunidadas de Castilla la Mancha,
Imprimir I dia 22 May 1999.

Campbell, Etta. *Linen Embroideries*. London, 1946.

Coats Sewing Group, J & P Coats Ltd. *Lagartera Embroidery*. Pillans & Wilson Ltd,
Glasgow, 1963.

Epstein, Kathleen. 'Concernynge the Excellency of the Nedle Worcke Spanisshe
Stitche'. *Piecework*, January/February 1995.

First Thread Your Needle. The Embroiderers' Guild of SA Inc., Mile End, SA, 1999.

Geddes, Elisabeth and McNeill, Moyra. *Blackwork Embroidery*. Dover Publications,
New York, 1976.

Lange, Jean. Class Notes: *Lagartera Embroidery*. The Embroiderers' Guild of SA Inc.,
Mile End, SA.

ACKNOWLEDGEMENT OF PIECES

The Publications Committee of The Embroiderers' Guild of SA Inc. would like to thank the following for their assistance and support in the production of this book: the Executive Committee of the Guild; Geoff Beale for photography; and Gunter Hanauer for the preparation of a number of the charts.

The Publications Committee comprised:

Jennifer Beale

Christine Bishop

Carol Mullan

Don Polson

Kerry Sanders

Gay Sanderson

Elisabeth Steinmetz

Jill Wadsworth

Carol Young

Embroideries and designs appearing in this book were provided by the following members of the Publications Committee:

Christine Bishop	Historical embroideries from personal collection
Carol Mullan	Motif sampler, Carnations, Tile designs, Border designs
Kerry Sanders	Novelty designs
Gay Sanderson	Violet Mat, Roumanian piece, Violet table runner
Chatelaine	Pin cushions and scissor fobs, Bookmarks
Elisabeth Steinmetz	Table mat
Jill Wadsworth	Endpapers: Sampler – dove's eye filling Alphabet sampler
Carol Young	Box top, Border Designs

The Embroiderers' Guild of South Australia Inc.
16 Hughes Street
Mile End SA 5031

Tel: (08) 8234 1104
Fax: (08) 8234 1513
Email: embguild@tne.net.au
Internet: www.embguildsa.org.au